All About Sports

All About
HOCKEY

BY MATT DOEDEN

Consultant:
Craig R. Coenen, PhD
Professor of History
Mercer County Community College
West Windsor, New Jersey

CAPSTONE PRESS
a capstone imprint

A+ Books are published by Capstone Press,
1710 Roe Crest Drive, North Mankato, Minnesota 56003
www.capstonepub.com

Library of Congress Cataloging-in-Publication Data
Doeden, Matt.
  All about hockey / by Matt Doeden.
      pages cm. — (A+ books. all about sports.)
  Includes bibliographical references and index.
  Summary: "Explains the game of hockey, including the game's
goals, positions, basic rules, and other points of interest"—
Provided by publisher.
  ISBN 978-1-4914-1996-0 (library binding)
  ISBN 978-1-4914-2173-4 (eBook PDF)
1. Hockey—Juvenile literature. I. Title.
  GV847.25.D64 2015
  796.355—dc23   2014027823

Editorial Credits
Brenda Haugen, editor; Sarah Bennett, designer; Eric Gohl,
media researcher; Katy LaVigne, production specialist

Photo Credits
Bridgeman Images: © British Library Board. All Rights Reserved/
British Library, London, UK, 6; Dreamstime: Jerry Coli, 10 (inset),
20, 27 (top), 28 (right), Michael Pettigrew, 24, Photographer2222,
cover; Getty Images: Bruce Bennett Studios, 9 (bottom), Focus
On Sport, 26 (right), Hulton Archive, 7 (top), NHLI/Mitchell
Layton, 12–13, Transcendental Graphics, 7 (bottom), 29 (top);
Library of Congress: 8, 9 (top); Newscom: Cal Sport Media/Kostas
Lymperopoulos, 27 (bottom), Cal Sport Media/Louis Lopez,
28 (left), Icon SMI/Allan Hamilton, 17 (right), Icon SMI/John
McDonough, 26 (left), Icon SMI/Matthew Pearce, 16, Icon SMI/
Minas Panagiotakis, 29 (bottom), Icon SMI/Rich Kane, 17 (left),
Icon Sportswire/Robin Alam, 23; Shutterstock: Digital Storm, 1,
Domenic Gareri, 15 (bottom), Iurii Osadchi, 4–5, 14, 21, 25 (top),
Laszlo Szirtesi, 10–11, 15 (top), Lorraine Swanson, 2–3, Papik, 19,
PhotoStock10, 25 (bottom), Pressmaster, 18, Sergey Lavrentev, 32,
Tumar, 30–31, Vladislav Gajic, 22

Design Elements: Shutterstock

Note to Parents, Teachers, and Librarians
This All About Hockey book uses full color photographs and a
nonfiction format to introduce the concept of hockey. All About
Hockey is designed to be read aloud to a pre-reader or to be
read independently by an early reader. Photographs help listeners
and early readers understand the text and concepts discussed.
The book encourages further learning by including the following
sections: Table of Contents, Glossary, Read More, Internet Sites,
and Index. Early readers may need assistance using these features.

Printed in the United States of America in
North Mankato, Minnesota
102014   008482CGS15

TABLE OF CONTENTS

GOAL!

A skater streaks down the ice. She spins around a defender and fires a shot. The goalie raises her glove, but the puck sails over it.

Goal! This is the thrilling sport of hockey.

ПОЖАЛОВАТЬ НА XXII ОЛИМПИЙСКИЕ ЗИМНИЕ ИГРЫ В СОЧИ

SOCHI 2014

THE BEGINNING

No one is sure where ice hockey was invented. It probably started with a stick-and-ball game such as field hockey.

Some say ice hockey started in English schoolyards. Others think it was invented in Canada. Or it may have come from Iceland.

THE RISE OF HOCKEY

Hockey grew more popular in the late 1800s and early 1900s.

Canadian J. G. Creighton loved the sport. He published the first ice hockey rules in 1877.

The National Hockey League (NHL) was born in 1917. Ice hockey became an Olympic sport three years later.

First American Olympic hockey team

The NHL started with only Canadian teams. The first U.S. team was the Boston Bruins. The Bruins joined the league in 1924.

Boston Bruins goalie Tiny Thompson in the 1930s

FACE-OFF

A game starts with a **face-off**. One player from each team stands at center ice. The referee drops the puck. The players battle for control. The team that gets the puck races toward the other team's goal. The other team tries to stop them from scoring.

Fact

Referees help run a hockey game. They start and stop the action and call **penalties**.

face-off—when the referee drops the puck between one player from each team; a face-off is used to start play at the beginning of the game or after play has been stopped

penalty—punishment a player gets when he or she breaks a rule of the game; the player then has to sit in the penalty box for two or more minutes

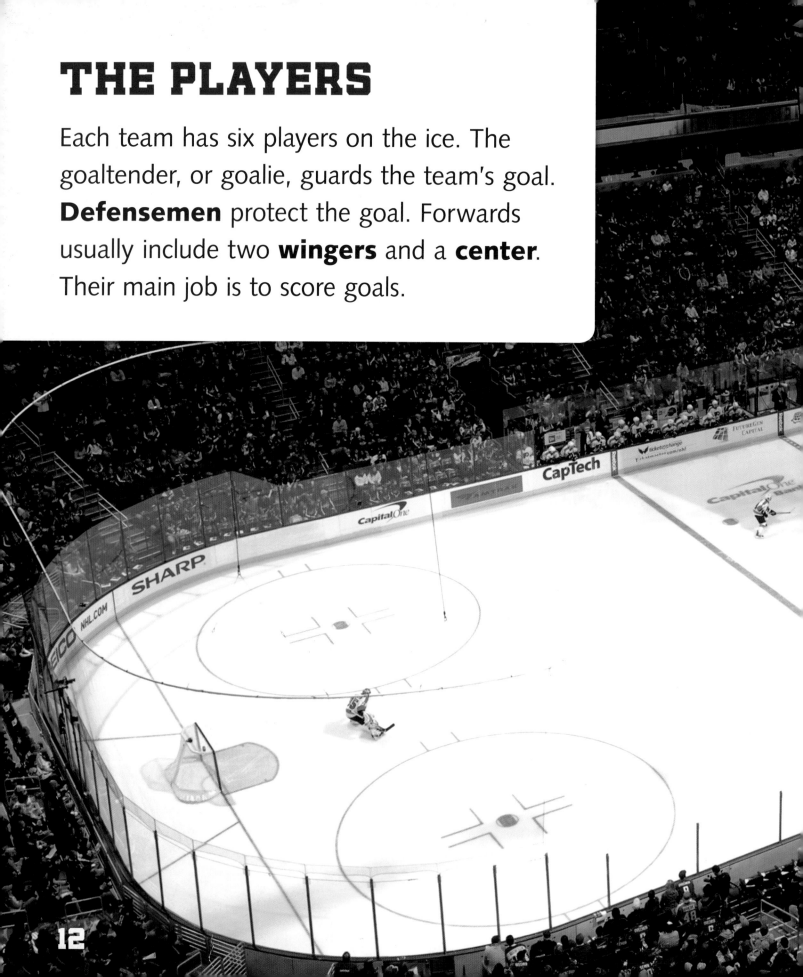

THE PLAYERS

Each team has six players on the ice. The goaltender, or goalie, guards the team's goal. **Defensemen** protect the goal. Forwards usually include two **wingers** and a **center**. Their main job is to score goals.

20:00
PENALTY 0 comcast 0 PENALTY
CAPITALS SPORTSNET FLYERS
SHOTS 0 PER SHOTS 0
1

goalie

defensemen

winger

center

winger

defenseman—a player who lines up in a defensive zone to prevent opponents from getting open shots on goal

winger—a type of forward who usually stays near the sides of the zone

center—the player who takes part in a face-off at the beginning of play

WINNING THE GAME

Players score goals by shooting the puck into the other team's net. The team that scores the most goals is the winner.

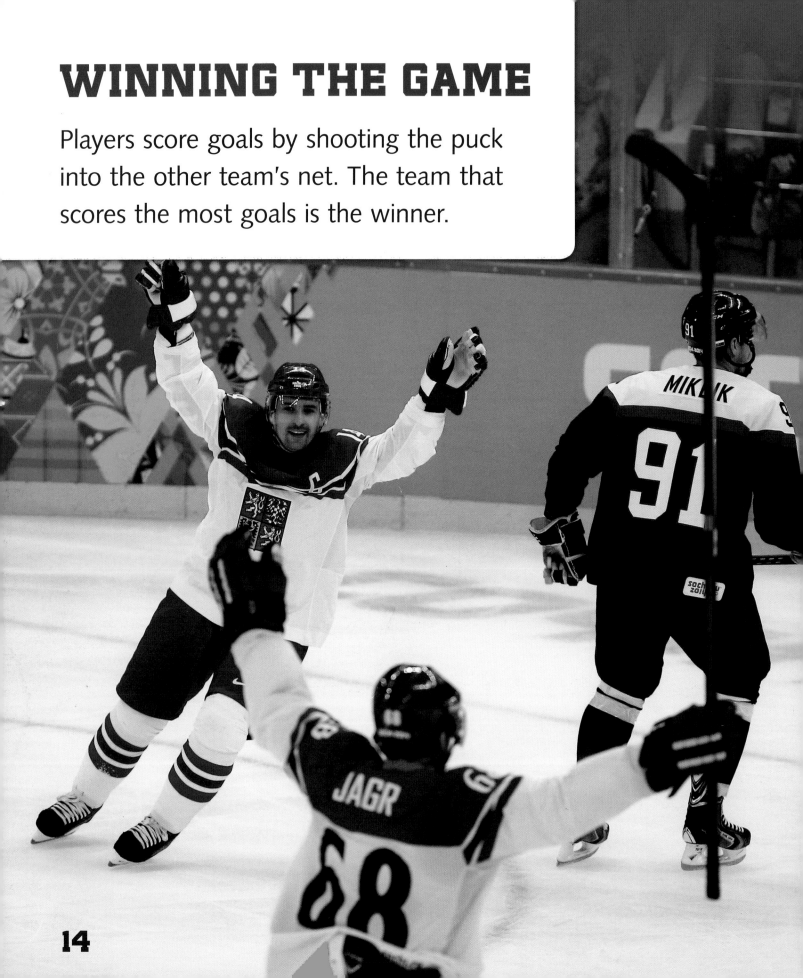

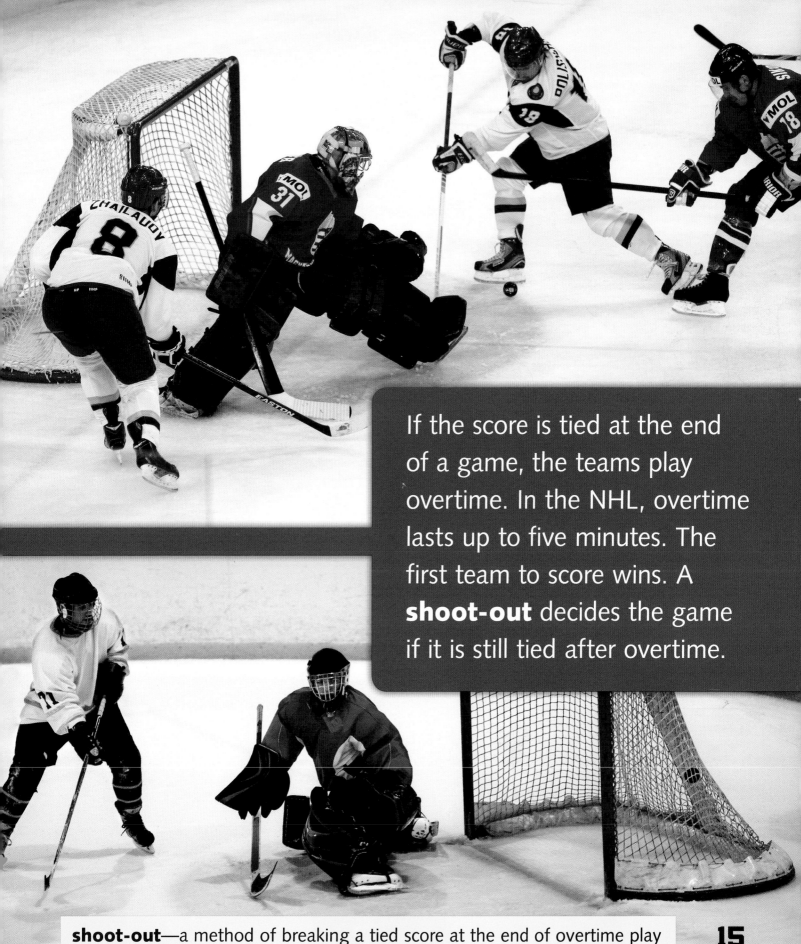

If the score is tied at the end of a game, the teams play overtime. In the NHL, overtime lasts up to five minutes. The first team to score wins. A **shoot-out** decides the game if it is still tied after overtime.

shoot-out—a method of breaking a tied score at the end of overtime play

POWER PLAY

Thweeeet!

The referee blows a whistle. A player is being called for a penalty. A penalty can be anything from tripping another player to fighting.

During a penalty, the player who broke the rules goes to the penalty box. The other team has more players on the ice. This is a **power play**. Most power plays last two minutes.

power play—when one team has more players on the ice because the other team has one or more players in the penalty box

17

SKATES

You can't play hockey without some gear. It starts with ice skates. They include a leather or plastic boot.

A sharp, single blade is attached to the bottom.

Most skates come up to a player's shins.

PUCKS AND STICKS

The puck is made of hard rubber. The top and bottom are smooth. The puck must slide easily over the ice.

Fact

The first hockey pucks were made of wood. Later, players made pucks by cutting flat sides on rubber balls.

Snap! A player takes a pass from a teammate. The puck makes a loud clicking sound as it hits the hockey stick.

Hockey sticks are long and thin. They have curved blades. Goalies use shorter, wider sticks.

21

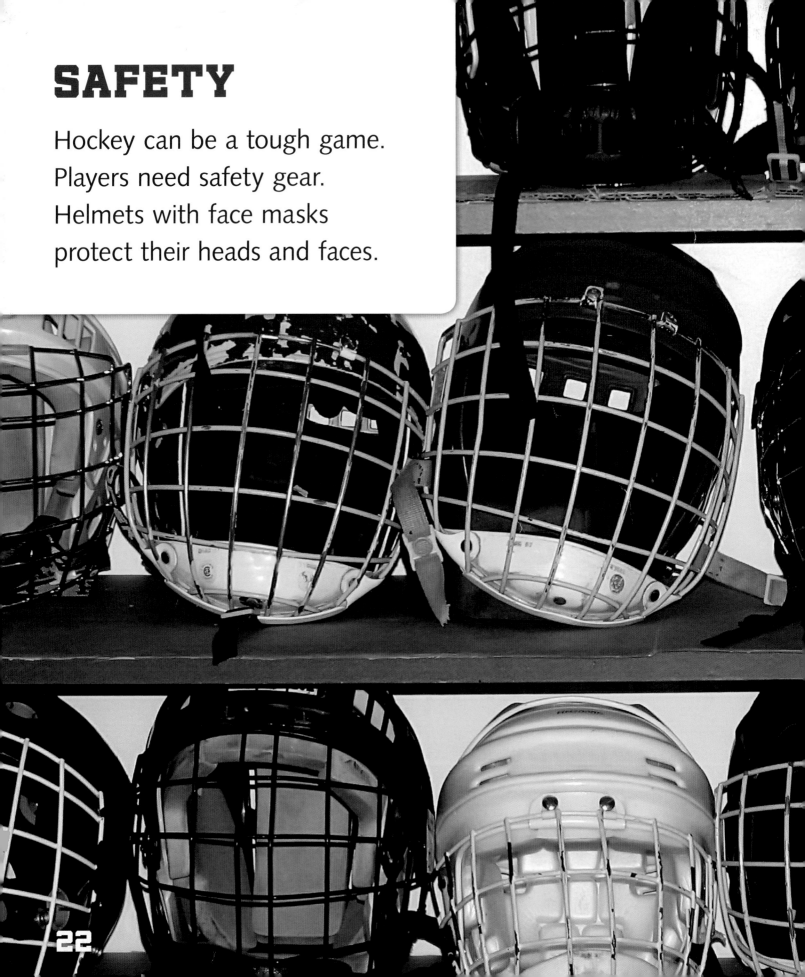

SAFETY

Hockey can be a tough game.
Players need safety gear.
Helmets with face masks
protect their heads and faces.

Pads cover most of a player's body.
Players wear shoulder pads, elbow pads,
and shin pads. They protect players
from speeding pucks and flying sticks.

GOALIE GEAR

Whoosh! A shot zips through the air so fast that it's hard to see. It doesn't fool the goalie. He reaches up and quickly grabs it. Goalies have special gear to protect them from flying pucks.

A goalie wears a large glove on one hand.

A padded blocker covers the other arm and the hand used to hold the stick.

A strong mask and throat protector keep the goalie's face and neck safe.

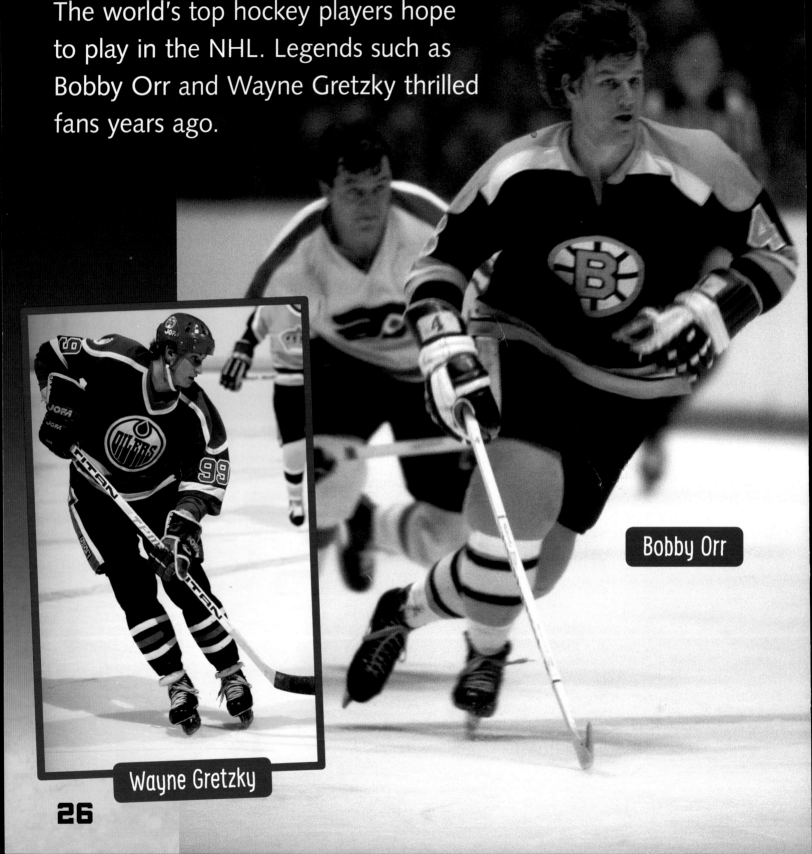

The world's top hockey players hope to play in the NHL. Legends such as Bobby Orr and Wayne Gretzky thrilled fans years ago.

Bobby Orr

Wayne Gretzky

Today fans love stars such as Sidney Crosby and Alexander Ovechkin.

Sidney Crosby

Alexander Ovechkin

27

THE STANLEY CUP

The Stanley Cup is pro hockey's biggest prize. The NHL champion wins this trophy. It takes a season of hard work. Every NHL player dreams of one day lifting the Stanley Cup.

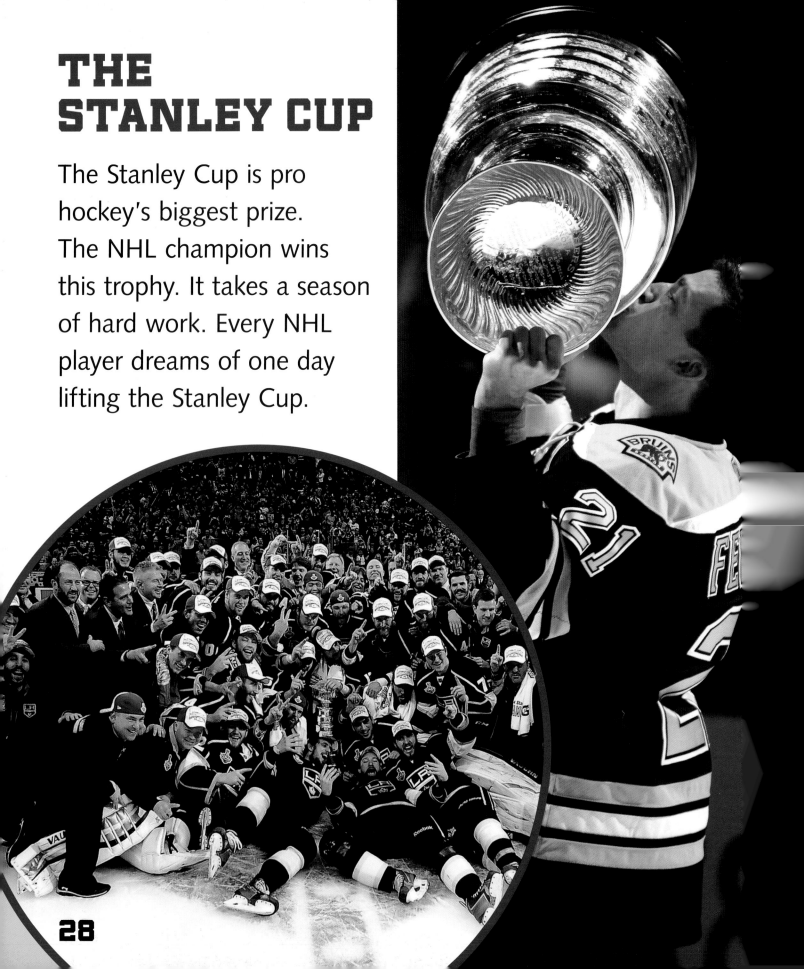

The Montreal Canadiens have won the Stanley Cup 23 times since the NHL formed. That is nearly twice as many as any other team!

GLOSSARY

center—the player who takes part in a face-off at the beginning of play

defenseman—a player who lines up in a defensive zone to prevent opponents from getting open shots on goal

face-off—when the referee drops the puck between one player from each team; a face-off is used to start play at the beginning of the game or after play has been stopped

penalty—punishment a player gets when he or she breaks a rule of the game; the player then has to sit in the penalty box for two or more minutes

power play—when one team has more players on the ice because the other team has one or more players in the penalty box

shoot-out—a method of breaking a tied score at the end of overtime play

winger—a type of forward who usually stays near the sides of the ice

READ MORE

Doeden, Matt. *Stars of Hockey.* Sports Stars. North Mankato, Minn.: Capstone Press, 2014.

Durrie, Karen. *Hockey.* Let's Play. New York: AV2 by Weigl, 2012.

Hurley, Michael. *Ice Hockey.* Fantastic Sports Facts. Chicago: Capstone Raintree, 2013.

INTERNET SITES

FactHound offers a safe, fun way to find Internet sites related to this book. All of the sites on FactHound have been researched by our staff.

Here's all you do:
Visit *www.facthound.com*
Type in this code: 9781491419960

Super-cool stuff! Check out projects, games and lots more at
www.capstonekids.com

INDEX